Old Lancashire Recipes

by

Joan Poulson

First edition – October, 1973
Second impression – March, 1974
Third impression February 1975

Published by Hendon Publishing Co. Ltd., Hendon Mill, Nelson, Lancashire.
Text © Joan Poulson 1973
Printed by Fretwell & Brian Ltd., Howden Hall, Silsden, Nr. Keighley, Yorkshire.

55p

Acknowledgements

I wish to thank all the friends and correspondents who have most generously loaned photographs, family recipe books and other material. Many libraries and organisations also gave me considerable help and I owe particular thanks to the following—

Ashton-Under-Lyne Public Library.
Bacup Public Library.
Bacup Natural History Society.
Blackburn Corporation.
Burnley Public Library.
Bury Public Library.
Colne Public Library.
Darwen Public Library.
Eccles Central Library.
The Leigh Library

Manchester Central Library.
Lancashire County Library, Preston.
Rochdale Libraries.
Southport Public Library.
St. Helens Central Library.
Warrington Municipal Library.
Widnes Public Library.
Wigan Public Library.
The City Engineers Photographic Section, Liverpool.

Introduction

LANCASHIRE housewives are among the best home cooks in the country and take pride in the fact that their county has always yielded good food.

This is mainly because Lancashire is a fertile county with a wide range of produce but I think it is also due to the fact that in the past Lancastrians have often had to make satisfying meals when not only money but food itself has been scarce. This has led, in many areas, to a heritage of careful cooking with the most value being obtained from any available food.

Since the Industrial Revolution, the county has become sub-divided into areas with particularly local dishes. In country districts the traditions of rich dishes involving large amounts of fresh cream, eggs, butter, etc. remain, but in more industrialised regions, dishes that were filling and economical while still tasty and nourishing, evolved. Many of these used very simple ingredients and could be left on the back of the hob for hours, or all day, while the family were all at the mill. They were welcomed home by the delicious aroma of hot-pot or weavers pudding and could 'set-to' immediately — if they were not too tired to eat.

This long, slow method of cooking, using the most basic of ingredients is also customary among the highly acclaimed peasant cooks of France.

Many traditional dishes originated in farmhouses but as the smallholders moved to towns after the Industrial Revolution, they had to adapt their culinary learning to produce meals from cheaper cuts of meat bought in shops.

Probably no other county has such a diversity of soils and climate and this means that the food is quite varied within the area.

From the flat, fertile plains of the west to the hilly north and east we get such delicious produce as Fylde fed pork, succulent pennine lamb, fresh salmon and trout and an enormous range of more homespun foods. These include tripe, black puddings, oatcakes, muffins and the best cooking cheese in the country.

During the 18th century the excellent quality cheese made in Lancashire was described as being 'superior to that of Cheshire'. Cheese made in the Leigh district was famed for its mildness and rich flavour, always gaining a high price in the markets.

As the 19th century saw the gradual rise of Southport as a centre for sea-bathing, it was reported in the Liverpool Courier that fish was very plentiful and that 'the lovers of good eating may abundantly gratify their appetites with turbot, salmon, sole, oysters, shrimps and sometimes with the john dory'.

The old custom of a dorval still continued at Easter-time in Southport when there was dancing, drinking and eating of fig pies.

Many traditional dishes have their origins in religious festivals. Feasting seems to have been essential at all such occasions and Shakespeare wrote 'Dost thou think, because thou art virtuous, there shall be no more cakes and ale'.

The baking of hot-cross buns at Easter seems to commemorate the cake baking of older, pagan festivities. Long ago, cakes and buns baked at Easter were supposed to have supernatural properties. A rhyme in Poor Robins Almanack for 1733 reads:-
    'Good Friday comes, the old woman runs
    With one or two a penny hot-cross buns,
    Whose virtue is, if you believe what's said,
    They'll not grow mouldy like the common bread'.

Some think that the cross on the buns was added when Christianity was first introduced into this country but others consider that it may have an even older derivation.

Simnel cakes are modern versions of ancient festive cakes. Herrick wrote:-
    "I'll to thee a simnel bring,
    Gainst thou go a-mothering;
    So that, when she blesses thee,
    Half that blessing thou'll give me."

Bury is noted for it's Simnel cakes, and the fourth Sunday in Lent was always kept as a festival.

It was written in 1873 that "An annual festival is held at Eccles, of great rustic celebrity and of high antiquity— The Eccles Wake commences on the Sunday— and consists (amongst many other things) of feasting upon a local confectionary called Eccles cakes, and ale, with various ancient and modern sports."

In 1879 it was reported that in the north of England, after the safe birth of a child, the doctor would cut up cake and cheese and everyone in the house would "partake of both, on pain of the poor baby growing up without personal charms."

In 19th century Lancashire though, few working class people would have been able to afford to have cake in the house much less pay a doctor to attend a normal child-birth.

There have always been differences in foods eaten by the rich and the very poor, but during this century this has been considerably less than during the 14th century when the poor existed on cheese, curds and therf cake (oat-cake) with the only vegetables being beans, leeks and cabbages. Only rarely was beef or pork eaten but wealthier people had a wide selection of game, fish and meat to give their meals variety.

A contemporary writer wrote in 1872 that "The poor of Cartmel parish ate no kind of bread but oatcake; neither was any beef killed except at Martinmas."

Edwin Waugh wrote of the period of famine in the cotton industry—"Blue milk (skimmed) and porridge were, for generations, the staple diet of the poorer worker."

An Oldham diarist wrote that he saw "scores of poor wretches" wandering around plucking nettles, water-cresses and docks and that nettles were being sold at 2d a pound. A nine-year old boy from Great Harwood wrote that he "went up and down seeking docks, which my mother boiled to make us a meal."

Bad harvests had added to the economic problems brought by the war and the years 1799–1801 were long remembered in Lancashire as 'The Barley Times' because few people could afford to buy corn. Very often meal and corn were bad as well as expensive.

When available however, porridge was popular throughout the county, and still is. It is sometimes eaten with syrup which could have its origins in the days when treacle balls were dropped into the sour oatmeal to sweeten it.

One record of a hundred years ago describes breakfast as "thick porridge and ale dip, with bread and cheese afterwards to fill up the corners."

An elderly woman living in Burnley told me that as one of a family of nine her mother had always to try to give them filling as well as nourishing meals. She remembers being given stirabout for breakfast and as a special treat, for supper, for "if you were full of warm food you slept better." To make it, good beef dripping is melted in a frying pan then boiling water poured in. Next stir in two tablespoons of syrup, or to taste, and mix until it dissolves. Keeping the pan over a very low heat (this would originally have been cooked over the fire) sprinkle in 'enough' oatmeal and stir until it is cooked, using a knife. Then serve it in a bowl as it is or with hot milk.

It is interesting to discover the similarities between dishes of various counties and even countries. Black puddings, popular in Lancashire, are rarely seen in southern counties yet a very similar food is eaten in France and called 'bondin' or blood pudding. Again, with tripe, a food uncommon in southern shops but in parts of France there are annual competitions for the best tripe dishes.

Tripe has been enjoyed in England for centuries and was regarded as a great delicacy by the Romans. Shakespeare mentioned it and of course it is a cheap source of good food value.

In medieval days, a dish called Tripe Normandy was made in Autumn when the pigs were killed as tripe and ham were the main ingredients. It is a dish that was probably brought to this country by William the Conqueror and is interesting because an important item in the recipe is a bay-leaf. (The French chef Escoffier included a bay-leaf in his recipe for English-style tripe.)

A wide variety of herbs and spices are used in old recipes including garlic, marjoram, bay-leaves and dill.

In the 13th century pork gravy was often preferred when coloured yellow with saffron, and rose-hips were preserved in 1730.

It was known that to draw a head of elderflowers through any jam or preserve would flavour it 'most delicately' and would add an extra and pleasant taste to cooked gooseberries.

Marjoram was used in farmhouse cooking between the 15th and 17th centuries, particularly to flavour milk and curd dishes and many old sweet recipes I found, contained rose-water.

Frequently though, the herbs used in meat cookery were to disguise the tainted meat.

A national dislike for herbs in cookery has lasted from the 18th century when the old country recipes were spoiled when they became popular in the homes of the upper classes, because of too lavish a use of herbs. During the past two decades, the enjoyment of Continental foods has brought a revival in their use.

The popularity of French dishes seems to indicate the quality of Lancashire foods which are often similar yet not known outside their native county. In a way, the wheel has come full circle, for the use of herbs and spices is again fairly general and it is quite fashionable to seek out small country inns specialising in Lancashire foods.

Here, one can enjoy such Lancastrian fare as black peas, brawn, hot-pot and deliciously light suet puddings, all in lavishly decorated old halls and inns. Quite a contrast to the grim hovels where such dishes were devoured hungrily in past days.

Very different to black peas are some of the items on the 16th century order sent from the Shuttleworths of Gawthorpe Hall, Padiham to a London merchant. They included 'comfits of almond, coriander, aniseed, cinnamon, ginger, marchpanes, macaroons, larks, sparrows, plovers, red shanks, thrushes, teales and mallards.'

Marchpanes, which were a fashionable part of a banquet, were biscuits made from sugar and almonds. They were served during a banquet given on Sunday, August 21st 1597 for the Earl and Countess of Derby, by the warden of Manchester, Dr. John Dee. The choicest wine was served and the table was spread with sweetmeats. The marchpanes were made in decorative shapes of men, animals, houses, etc.

Very often at such banquet the marchpanes would be in the shape of a castle which the ladies and gentlemen broke into pieces by besieging it 'in frolic' with sugar plums.

Some of the recipes in this book are very old and are included because I find them interesting and hope that you will. Others are of more recent origin and are more suitable for cooking today, but they have all been discovered during research or were sent to me by someone living in the towns shown in the adjoining photograph.

This was mainly intended to be a book of old recipes and customs connected with Lancashire dishes. I planned to include a few photographs to show where these foods had come from but became so interested and absorbed by them that their part in the book 'just growed.'

So it really became a Lancashire gobbet. This is an archaic word meaning a piece, or taste, of food, and my book is offered as just a taste of the many interesting old recipes and bits of information I have discovered from our county.

JOAN POULSON

Lancashire Scallops

The word scallops is a corruption of the French 'escalope' and usually means veal but can sometimes refer to young lamb. In Lancashire it has come to mean a dish of peeled, chopped onion and thinly sliced potato with rashers of lean or streaky bacon cut up without rind. Smoked bacon gives a very good flavour. These ingredients are put into a casserole in layers ending with potatoes, then water added to about $\frac{1}{2}''$ below the level of the top potatoes. The casserole is lidded and put into a medium hot oven, 375° about 1 hour. The lid can be removed during the last 20 minutes of cooking to brown the potatoes but take care that the dish does not dry too much.

Lancashire Spice Parkin

4 oz flour	$\frac{1}{4}$ teaspoon bicarbonate
4 oz fine oatmeal	of soda
4 oz demerara sugar	2 oz syrup
$\frac{1}{4}$ teaspoon mixed spice	2 oz treacle
4 tablespoons milk	$\frac{1}{2}$ an egg
	2 oz lard

Mix the flour, oatmeal and spice. Melt the sugar, lard, treacle and a little of the milk. Beat the egg well and add that. Mix it all to a stiff batter and add the bicarbonate of soda dissolved in the remaining milk. Mix quickly and put into a well greased tin about 5″ by 9″. Cook in a moderate oven 325°-350° until firm.

Market Street, Leigh in the late 19th century. The beef and bacon, hanging outside the shops, looks unhygienic but certainly more picturesque than plastic wrapped, frozen cubes of meat. It was in 1880, incidentally, that the first cargoes of frozen meat arrived in this country from abroad.

Leigh now possesses a fine new library and art gallery but few buildings of any historical interest remain in the town.

Lancashire Cheese Scones

8 oz S.R. flour	1 oz butter
4 oz Lancs. cheese	$\frac{1}{4}$ teaspoon salt
$\frac{1}{4}$ pt. milk	$\frac{1}{2}$ teaspoon dry mustard

Sift together the flour, salt and mustard. Rub in the butter to give a texture of fine crumbs. Grate the cheese and add 3 oz to the mixture then bind to a soft dough with milk. Roll on a floured board to $\frac{1}{2}''$ thick and cut into rounds. Place on a greased baking tray, brush with milk and sprinkle with the remaining cheese. Bake 12 minutes in a hot oven 425° Mark 7.

These scones are very good with salads or with savoury dishes.

Old Herb Cheese

8 oz Lancs. cheese	3 tablespoons sack
1 oz butter	(sweet sherry)
4 tablespoons single cream	2 tablespoons mixed
or top of the milk	chopped herbs—sage,
	chives, parsley, thyme.

Crumble the cheese finely and put all the ingredients into a heat-proof bowl over a pan of simmering water. Stir until creamy and pour into small pots. Cover when cold and keep in a cool place.

Dried herbs can be used but only half the given amount.

The name Leigh comes from the Anglo-Saxon leah, meaning a pasture or meadow, and the area around the town was a rich grassland. The cheese produced there was sometimes described as 'the Leigh Cheese' and later 'the Leigh Toaster' because of its excellence in all cooking and especially for toasting. Cheese has not been made commercially in the Leigh area since the mid-nineteenth century.

Quite a congested scene on Market Street, Manchester in 1900, the year of the Relief of Mafeking.
This was a period when, despite the improvement in road surfaces, city shopping was not particularly pleasant because of the smell from horse droppings.

Manchester Pudding (1888)

3 oz breadcrumbs	3 tablespoons brandy
½ pint milk	a strip of lemon peel
4 eggs	sugar to taste
2 oz butter	Puff pastry
Jam	

Put the lemon peel into the milk and warm gently then leave for 30 minutes. Strain the milk on to the breadcrumbs, bring to the boil and cook for 2 or 3 minutes. Beat the egg yolks and two of the whites. Add these with the butter, sugar and brandy. Stir them well together. Put the puff pastry into a prepared dish, cover with a thick layer of jam and pour the mixture in when it is cold. Bake the pudding for an hour in a moderate oven, (325°-350°). Serve it cold with a little sifted sugar sprinkled over.

Hot Cakes

8 oz S.R. flour	1 tablespoon castor sugar
1 oz butter	1 egg
1 oz lard	milk to mix

Rub the fats in the flour and mix in the sugar. Beat the egg and stir in with a little milk if necessary to give a firm paste. Roll out thickly and cut into rounds. Bake in a hot oven 425° until nicely brown. Butter and serve hot.

I have been told that these were always served in one farmhouse for breakfast but they really must be eaten while still hot and fresh.

Potato Pastry

8 oz plain flour	2 oz butter
4 oz sieved, cooked potato	2 oz lard
½ teaspoon salt	water to mix

Sift the flour and salt in a basin, rub in the fats and add the potato. Mix lightly with a little cold water to make a very dry dough. Roll out thinly and use for sweet or savoury dishes but it is especially good for meat pies, sausages rolls, etc.

This photograph taken in Eccles in the late 19th century, is of Wardles shop which sold 'the original Eccles Cakes', but is not the building where the first cakes were made. It also sold ice-cream, at ½d. and 1d a glass, and herb beer.

The thatched building is interesting, not least because of the rather unlikely date given for its erection but it was demolished to make way for the building of a bank in 1915.

One noteworthy detail is the poster on the wall. It advertises a circus and the bill is headed by Houdini, the world-famous escapologist.

Eccles Cakes

It is believed that these cakes had a religious significance similar to that of the shewbread placed upon the altar of the Temple by the Hebrews.

When the Puritans forbade dancing on the village green, together with all public festivities, the eating of cakes at religious festivals came under the ban. Eccles had a particularly stern Puritan parson but oddly enough Eccles Cakes continued to be baked. They were later sold at many of the fairs and wakes in Lancashire.

Eccles Cakes should be shining and moist inside with a glossy, golden, sticky outside.

1 lb flaky pastry	2 oz candied peel
1 oz melted butter	4 oz sugar
Nutmeg	8 oz currants

Roll the pastry thinly and cut into rounds. Thoroughly mix the ingredients and place on the rounds. Dampen the edges and gather together. Flatten and snip a V in the top with scissors. Brush with water and sprinkle with sugar. Bake in a hot oven for 20 minutes. 425°. Gas Mark 7.

An Excellent Keep Cake from Ulverston

8 oz butter	Grated rind ½ lemon
8 oz castor sugar	4 oz raisins
8 oz flour	4 oz sultanas
2 oz ground almonds	4 oz cherries (chopped)
1 tablespoon brandy	2 oz citron peel
2 oz rice flour (or ground rice)	5 eggs
	1 heaped teasp. baking powder

Beat the butter for 5 minutes. Add the sugar and rind, beat another 5 minutes. Add the beaten yolks of the eggs and the brandy, beat 10 minutes. Continue beating and add the fruit, almonds, cherries, raisins and peel. Stir in the stiffly whipped egg whites alternately with the sieved flour, rice flour and baking powder. Add them in small amounts and mix well then turn into a well greased, lined tin and bake for 2 hours in a moderate oven 325°-350°.

This is a most delicious cake but without the help of an electric food mixer you might well need a glass of an old-fashioned Pick-Me-Up after the prolonged beating. But even if you do use a mixer—try some and spoil yourself!

Brandy Cordial

¼ pt. brandy	¼ pt. thick barley water
3 egg yolks	castor sugar to taste
1 tablespoon cream	

Beat the yolks and cream together. Add the barley water and brandy. Stir briskly and sweeten. Strain and bottle. Use a few teaspoons in cases of weakness.

Pick-Me-Up

2 fresh eggs	¼ pt. rum
2 large lemons	½ pt. milk
4 oz sugar	

Put the eggs and shells (which will dissolve) in a basin, squeeze lemon juice over and scrape pulp on top. Cover and keep airtight 5 days. Mix well with milk and rum and pour into clean, dry bottles. Cork tightly and use a wineglassful each morning–in a little warm water if liked.

Damson Cheese

This is a delicacy from Georgian days and was mentioned in Parson Woodruffes diary in the 18th century. It was sometimes taken as a present when invited out to tea.

Put the damsons into a stone jar, cover and put into a very slow oven until the juice runs freely and the stones are loose. Stir well and rub through a sieve then crack the stones and add the kernels to the fruit pulp. Put this into a pan and to each pound of pulp add a pound of warm sugar. Bring to the boil slowly and then boil well until it will set. Pour into warm pots, cover with a paper dipped in brandy then top cover. Damson Cheese is best left to mature for a few months and makes a rich sweet when served with fresh cream and port.

Cottage Pie

1 lb minced beef
1 lb mashed potato
1 level tablespoon flour
1 small onion
1 teasp. chopped parsley
1 teasp. Worcester sauce
$\frac{1}{4}$ pt. hot gravy or beef stock

Heat a little fat in a frying pan and fry the beef and onion until brown then thoroughly mix in the flour. Gradually stir in the liquid and add the parsley and sauce. Put all this into a casserole and cover with the potato. Bake in a moderate oven until the top is golden brown, about $\frac{3}{4}$ hr.

A photograph, probably taken at the end of the last century outside The Manor House, Scholes, Wigan. Little is known of the history of this building but, in the past, homes of well to do farmers were often called manor houses, and perhaps this is the origin of the name here. It is said that in 1862, the house was besieged for some days 'to the excitement of the town'.

Here are some of the women typical of working class families in Lancashire at that time, dressed in clogs and shawls. These were both practical and comfortable. Practical, since they were cheap and hard-wearing and comfortable in that they were warm and easy to wear. At least, the clogs were when they had been 'broken in' but many childrens ankles bled before they reached the stage of comfort.

Lancashire Foot

A Lancashire Foot is similar to a very thick pasty but is elliptical in shape to fit into the tins that miners used to carry their snappin or snap down the pit. The oval-section tins were found to be most convenient in the cramped conditions.

The name 'Foot' was given because of the shape and the miners wife or mother would usually make a pair, not only because it is as easy to make two as one, given the ingredients, but because a Foot was a popular snappin.

Apparently the plural was not Feet but Foots! A sentence from a story in a magazine of 1900 reads 'She's left his Foots in t'oven and they're burnt to cinders'.

The pastry was rolled into a long oval and cut lengthways into two, then the rolling-pin placed halfway along the length and the pastry just rolled from the centre to the further edge. This gave the 'foot' shape, with the heel nearer to the cook and the sole widening out at the top edge. It was a simple but effective way of keeping the base crust thick and the upper one thin but also larger to cover the filling.

Meat was not always used, sometimes the filling would consist of egg or cheese. This is also a possible origin of the Lancashire fondness for cheese and onions, either raw or cooked in pies and pasties.

The Filling—to 1 lb of shortcrust pastry, a mixture of $\frac{3}{4}$ lb lean beef cut up small, 2 or 3 medium sized potatoes peeled and diced and 1 large onion peeled and sliced thinly. This mixture is seasoned and cooked with a little water in a slow oven until the meat is tender. Then when cold it is used to fill the pastry. The Foots are then baked until brown at 375° or Gas Mark 5.

One of the earliest photographs in this book. Bridge Street, St. Helens, taken from the Liverpool Road end in 1887. Just thirty years before this, in 1856, the Crimean War ended, so it is possible that some of the men in this photograph would have fought in the war.

I particularly like the magnificent street lamp in the foreground and wonder if it is still preserved in St. Helens.

Colliers Foot

Colliers Foot is shaped like the Lancashire Foot (recipe on page 17) but bacon fat is traditionally used to mix the pastry and a little is also spread over the 'heel' part after rolling out. The filling consists of a layer of thinly sliced onion then finely sliced cheese and topped with a slice of bacon. As each layer is placed on the pastry it is seasoned, the onions with salt, the cheese with pepper and the bacon with a sprinkle of dry mustard. The top is folded over, edges dampened and firmly sealed. Bake 375° Gas Mark 5 until golden brown.

Sometimes, to give an even more moist filling, a spoonful of beer or broth was put over the filling or a slice of apple added. If there was an egg to spare, this might be beaten with a little milk and seasoned, then half poured over each foot.

A modern savoury having similar ingredients to the Colliers Foot but having better keeping qualities is the Lancashire Cheese Savoury.

Lancashire Cheese Savoury

8 oz Lancashire cheese crumbled finely	4 rashers of streaky bacon
1 small onion	

Mince the onion and bacon or chop very finely and mix thoroughly with the cheese to a well-blended paste. Add pepper to taste as you mix. Keep well covered in the 'fridge until required then toast one side of fairly thick slices of bread. Turn, spread the cheese savoury on the untoasted side and grill very slowly, or preferably put into a hot oven for about 15 minutes or until the cheese has puffed up and is lightly browned.

The savoury will keep for a week in the 'fridge.

Pickled Red Cabbage

1 firm, medium sized cabbage	2 pints vinegar
2 level teaspoons allspice	salt
2 level teaspoons peppercorns	

Quarter the cabbage, removing the outer leaves and centre stalk then cut each quarter very finely into strips. Put them into a bowl, sprinkle well with salt and leave until next day. Put the peppercorns and allspice into a piece of muslin and boil in the vinegar. Take off the heat and after 2 hrs. remove the bag of spices. Drain the cabbage well on the second day, put in jars and cover with the cold vinegar then tie down.

Bowland Tart

1½-2 oz coconut	1 oz cherries
1 egg, beaten	an uncooked flan case

Chop the cherries and mix into the egg with enough coconut to make a loose paste. Spread in the pastry case.

4 oz sugar	1 oz S.R. flour
4 oz butter	2 oz wholemeal flour
1 egg	1 oz custard powder

Cream the butter and sugar. Sift the flours and custard powder together and add to the sugar mixture alternately with the beaten egg. Put into the flan, decorate the edges and bake 375° for ½ hr or until golden brown.

Potato Cakes

These are a traditional Lancashire savoury but are also known in other parts of the country where they are sometimes called potato scones or potato bread.

Into hot, well seasoned, mashed potatoes stir a large knob of butter and mix it in well. Then stir in some top of the milk and enough flour to give a manageable dough. Quantities could be — 1 lb cooked potatoes, 2 oz butter, about 4 oz of flour and 1 or 2 tablespoons of top of the milk. These are not exact amounts because a lot depends on the type of potato. Flatten and cut into small rounds $\frac{1}{4}$-$\frac{1}{2}$″ thick (the thinner one will make a crisper potato cake) and bake on a hot, greased griddle. Turn when brown on the under side and serve hot and buttered. They can also be cooked on a greased oven tray in a hot oven.

Sweet Potato Cake

A delicious variation for tea on 'back end' days but sadly, very fattening.

Just make the potato cakes as usual but cut to about $\frac{3}{4}$″. When cooked on both sides split open and lay a slice of butter inside. Sprinkle well with sugar (preferably brown) and close, then put into a dish. Keep them hot until you have cooked them all, when you will find that you not only have the potato cakes to enjoy but also the appetising 'sauce' that has oozed out.

A sunny day outside The Old Thatched Inn, The Rock, Bury. The date of this photograph is uncertain, but the inn was demolished in 1886. The boy on the right seems to have been pleased to rest from pushing his cart. He was probably out at work from an early age. The girl in the centre is wearing the clogs and shawl which were almost a uniform among the poor of Lancashire, and her tattered clothes certainly mark her as that.

Not so common was the tam o' shanter which was worn by the bearded man on the left of the photograph.

Simnel Cake (Bury Knob Simnel)

The word simnel has been spelled symnell, symnel and simbling in the past. One school of thought says that it is derived from the Anglo-Saxon symel and symbel, meaning a feast and another that it comes from the word Siminellus, which was a Roman festive bread eaten during the Spring fertility rites, the Latin word simila meaning fine flour.

A traditional story says that the father of Lambert Simnel, the pretender to Henry VIII, was the famous baker of these cakes which have retained his name. An interesting theory but incorrect as there were references to Simnel Cakes many years before this period.

There is no doubt though, that these cakes were made for the fourth Sunday in Lent, known as Mothering Sunday, as a welcome release from the austerities of the season. This special day was originally to honour the Mother Church at Jerusalem but became the day on which servant girls were allowed to go home to visit their mothers. The mistress of the house would allow them to bake a cake to take home and this was usually a Simnel Cake.

For many years it has been more of an Easter Cake but has always been a speciality of the Bury area. Now it is very often decorated with icing, coloured eggs and chickens instead of the traditional marzipan with marzipan 'knobs'. These balls, incidentally, are supposed to have originated in the days when Mothering Sunday was to honour the Mother Church and are to represent the apostles of Jesus who founded the first church.

An old Bury recipe for a Simnel Cake—

12 oz S.R. flour	6 oz currants
6 oz brown sugar	6 oz raisins
4 oz butter	2 oz ground almonds
2 oz lard	2 eggs
1 teaspoon nutmeg	$\frac{1}{2}$ teasp. mixed spice

Cream the butter and sugar thoroughly, add the well beaten eggs alternately with the flour and then stir in the fruits and spice.

Cream the fats and sugar thoroughly, and in a separate bowl mix the flour, spices and almonds. Stir these dry ingredients into the creamed mixture alternately with the well beaten eggs. Mix in the fruit and two tablespoons of rum or brandy if liked. Put into a prepared tin and bake in a moderate oven 325° for 30 minutes, then reduce the heat to 300° for a further 1½-2 hrs.

When cool, brush with warmed apricot jam, cover with marzipan and make balls or egg shapes with some and set them around the edge. If more colour is required, brush with beaten egg white, dust with caster sugar and put into a cool oven for 30 minutes.

This photograph of Bacup shows one of the first steam trams in the town. They were introduced in 1889 and although there is a lot of interest being shown in the tram, the photographer has aroused considerable curiosity. He cannot have been a common sight in those days.

Lancashire Hot-Pot

Hot-Pot was always made from mutton in the past but now appears to be popular when made from beef. The name comes from the pot in which the dish was cooked. These were very deep earthenware containers in brown or white and often had the words Hot-Pot written on the side.

Incredible as it might now appear, oysters were often included in this dish for when it originated they cost very little. (Dr. Johnsons cat Hodge was fed on them for 2d. a day).

Very often too, kidneys or black puddings were added but whatever the ingredients, Hot-Pot is always served from the dish in which it is cooked, and it is traditional to serve pickled red cabbage with this meal. This is probably to counter-act the richness of the meat with the sharp tang of the pickle.

While we now tend to make Hot-Pot in layers, probably because the traditionally shaped pots are not easy to obtain, the original method was to stand the mutton chops on end in the pot. Since the large Pennine sheep had long chop bones, the initial pots had to be tall and straight to hold them, with well-fitting lids to retain the moisture and flavour.

The oldest Hot-Pot recipe I have is the following—

'Make a big brown earthenware hot pot with a fitted lid right hot. Put a bayleaf in a spoonful of dripping at the bottom. Get some mutton chops and flour and pepper them, then fry them brown on both sides. Take them out and pack them into the pot standing on their heads, thin ends up. If the chops had a kidney put that in too.

Chop up an onion for each chop, fry and pack it among the chops. Take a few carrots, chop and flour them then brown in the fat and pack them among the onions. Peel some potatoes and cut them into thick slices then put them on top, overlapping them like slates on a roof. Pepper and salt as you go and if you can get a dozen oysters put them under the potatoes (don't fry these).

Now take the fat you have fried all in, thicken it with flour and stir until brown, pour in boiling water and stir until this gravy is well cooked. Season it with pepper and salt and then a good sprinkle of sugar (do not leave this out).

Pour in the gravy till it comes to the level of the potatoes, put on the lid and bake with a good fire for 2 hours. Ten minutes before dinner take off the lid, rake up the fire and get the potatoes 'right brown.'

Oatmeal Scrapple

This is an updated version of an old recipe calling for 3 lb lean pork, etc. but I have found that this is still popular while being considerably more economical.

2 cups fine oatmeal 1 cup pork sausage meat
2½ cups water 1 teasp. salt

Bring the water to the boil and sprinkle in the salt and oatmeal, stirring constantly. Reduce the heat and simmer very gently 15 mins. or until thick. Keep stirring so that it does not stick. Mix in the meat thoroughly and press into a loaf tin or narrow dish. When cold, cover and leave overnight, then slice and dip into flour or breadcrumbs. Fry until brown on both sides in a little fat.

Old Treacle Roll

Roll some firm suet pastry into a long oblong and cover with fine white breadcrumbs, leaving a 2″ space around the edge. Sprinkle with lemon juice then cover with syrup. Wet the edges and roll up, sealing the edges together well to prevent the syrup from running out. Roll loosely in greaseproof paper then in a well floured cloth. Tie securely but leave the cloth fairly loose and put into a pan of boiling water and cook for 1¼ hours or longer if very large. Serve hot with custard or white sauce.

Pork Cheese

1 lb lean pork	3 teasp. salt
1 lb fat pork	1½ teasp. pepper
1 tablespoon chopped	1 teasp. chopped parsley
chives or spring onions	1 teasp. mixed sage and
	thyme

Mix all these ingredients well and press into a shallow tin. Bake slowly for one hour. Pour over it ½ pt. of aspic jelly made with a good bone stock. Allow to go cold and set.

This is very good served sliced with salad or it makes a good tea with home-made bread and pickles.

A good cut of pork to use is belly-pork, trimmed of its rind, since this is a good mixture of fat and lean meat so all the 2 lb of meat necessary can be this economical joint.

Jessies Loaf

8 oz S.R. flour	3 tablespoons honey
1 egg	3 oz margarine
½ cup milk	

Beat the egg well and mix thoroughly with the milk. Rub the margarine into the flour and stir in the liquid. Add the honey and mix all together very well. Put into a well greased tin and bake in a moderate oven 350° for 45 minutes or until firm. Serve sliced and buttered.

Warrington grew up around a river ford and in the 18th century was developing as a port. It was also famous for its seat of learning, The Warrington Academy and for the making of sail cloths.

This photograph was taken in the latter half of the 19th century, outside The Barley Mow Inn in Warrington Market Place. The little oyster stall standing outside was not a very unusual sight in those days when oysters could be bought for 6d.—1/- a dozen (2½p.–5 new pence).

Warrington Heavy Pudding

2 oz dried fruit	2 oz suet
3 oz flour	1 teasp. baking powder
2 oz sugar	grated rind ½ lemon
6 slices stale bread	pinch mixed spice

Put the bread in a bowl and cover with hot water. Leave until it is soft, then put in a sieve and leave to drain well. Put into a clean bowl, beat till smooth then add all the other ingredients together with a little milk to make a fairly stiff but moist mixture. Put into a well buttered basin and steam for 2½ hours.

Dormers

8 oz cold cooked beef	1 egg, beaten
2 oz suet	4 oz fresh breadcrumbs
3 oz boiled rice	parsley, chopped

Mince the meat and mix with the rice and suet and season to taste. Shape into rounds and dip into the egg then roll in the breadcrumbs. Fry until golden and serve with gravy.

One of the oldest ballads preserved in the Lancashire dialect contains a reference to 'snig poy', i.e. eel pie, made from eels caught in the River Mersey at Warrington. It dates from 1548 and mentions the bailiff to Sir Thomas Butler of the town.

The fourth verse relates—

An he gen me a lunchin o' denty snig poy,
An by th'hond did he shak me most lovingly.

When the market was removed from the main road in Colne in 1897, a new market was opened in Dockray Street and the open market transferred to this site nearby, being called 'Jews Alley'.

There is a marked contrast in dress here, between the beautifully frilled clothes of the child on the left and the little clogs and shawl worn by the girl in front of the stall.

Many fine old buildings have been destroyed in the town but modern development cannot alter the lovely setting of hills.

Clanger

Suet-crust pastry   approx. 8 oz lean bacon
  (using 8 oz flour,   1 onion
    4 oz suet, etc.)

Peel the onion and chop it very finely, cut up the bacon and remove the rind. Grease a basin and line with the pastry. Put the bacon into a frying pan over a very low heat to extract the fat, then allow it to brown gently. Take the bacon from the pan and put in a bowl. Fry the onion until golden then put it into the bowl with the bacon. Sprinkle in a little fresh parsley and sage and pepper to taste. Mix well then put into the pastry lined basin. Cover with a lid made from the left-over pastry and top with several layers of greaseproof paper. Steam for 2½ hours and serve with a green vegetable and perhaps grilled tomatoes. It is also delicious with freshly boiled beetroot and parsley sauce.

Bell-Ringers Flip

This was recommended to be drunk by the bell-ringers before a long peal. Probably as a boost to strength and energy as well as to wet the whistle.

Separate 8 eggs into two large bowls. Beat the whites until very stiff. Strain the juice from 2 or 3 oranges and beat into the yolks adding sugar to taste. Into this bowl put sweet spices of your choice, for example cinnamon, nutmeg and perhaps a pinch of ginger and beat together very well. Now slowly heat 2 pints of strong beer and when it is hot pour it slowly and from a good height onto the yolks. This should come to a good froth and should now have the whites stirred in before it is drunk, still hot.

A market day in Blackburn in 1906. The central figures would have had to stand motionless for several seconds while the photograph was taken. Some of the children seen would never have tasted grapes, which were a delicacy working class families could not have afforded. The baby being held in the foreground might well be living in Blackburn today.

Steak and Onions

1 lb shoulder steak	parsley
1 onion	flour
seasoning to taste	water or stock

Mix the flour with some pepper and dip the steak into it. Fry the onion in fat until soft and golden then put it into a shallow oven dish with the steak. Sprinkle with finely chopped parsley, salt and the liquid - about ¼ pint. Cook in a moderate oven 350° until tender. This will take about 1½-2 hours but check occasionally that it is not too dry. If this happens add a little hot liquid.

North Country Christmas Sweet Pie

I have had this recipe from various sources but each copy is almost identical to the others. One correspondent in Barrow-in-Furness calls it Old Fashioned Christmas Sweet Pie and told me that it was always made in farmhouses to be eaten after the Christmas dinner, and that it is still made in some areas.

puff pastry	2oz candied peel
½ lb fat mutton chops	juice of a large lemon
8 oz currants	pinch of salt
8 oz raisins	2 wineglasses rum
8 oz sultanas	ground nutmeg, mace,
6 oz soft brown sugar	pepper and cinnamon to taste

Cut the skin and bones from the meat and dice it. Mix all the other ingredients together and place in layers, with the meat alternating, in a dish. End with a layer of meat. Bake with a lid on the dish until tender—approx. 1 hour 350°, then cover with the pastry and bake at 425° until well risen and golden brown.

The Rev. W. B. Daniel listed the 'Bill Of Fare For Dinner' given by Earl Grosvenor to the Corporation of Chester in 1813. After an extensive list which included 8 boiled turkeys, 4 roasted turkeys, 4 geese, 10 haunches of venison and 20 moulds of jelly, etc. etc., he wrote "To this must be added, an imense Baron of Beef and a Christmas Pie weighing upwards of two hundred pounds."

Ormskirk Market over fifty years ago. One of the most noticeable features on this photograph of a bustling market is the absence of traffic. Traffic congestion was often as much of a problem in the days when ponies and carts were the only vehicles on the roads, as it is today, The difference being that parking spaces held carts and gigs while the horses needed stabling facilities.

Ormskirk Gingerbread

4 oz butter or margarine	2 level teaspoons ground ginger
6 oz sugar	$\frac{1}{4}$ lb syrup
1 level teasp. bicarbonate of soda	1 tablespoon milk
a pinch of salt	$\frac{1}{4}$ lb treacle
1 lb plain flour	

Blend the butter, sugar, ginger and bicarbonate of soda. Add the syrup, treacle and milk, then the flour and salt mixed. Knead together very thoroughly then roll out fairly thinly. Cut into rounds and bake in a moderate oven 350° Gas Mark 4 for 12-15 minutes.

This is a modern adaptation of an old recipe which is rather like a treacle version of brandy-snaps.

I include the old recipe since it is good, but do space out the drops widely since they spread and as they have to be curled while hot I suggest you do this around the handle of a wooden baking spoon.

10 oz flour	$\frac{1}{4}$ oz mace
12 oz butter	1 lb sugar
1 lb treacle	$\frac{1}{4}$ oz cinnamon
$\frac{1}{2}$ oz ground ginger	a little lemon rind, finely grated

Melt the butter and mix with the treacle and sugar. Add the flour, lemon and spices. Beat together and drop onto a greased tin. Bake in a moderate oven and leave until the edges are well set but the centres still bubbling. Take out of oven and turn each piece around your fingers.

A beautiful print of Lancaster in 1807 when roads were used mainly by carts and cattle but were badly surfaced. It was almost impossible, before the days of motor traffic, for pedestrains to cross roads without getting dusty or muddy, according to the weather.

Roads in larger towns were probably worst; the heavy horse drawn waggons constantly churning up the top surface and leaving an extra hazard for long skirts in the form of horse droppings.

Ale Gruel

This was a popular bedtime drink in more northerly areas and gives a lovely picture of a wife caring for her husband, but not much in tune with todays Womens Lib. ideals.

When a man arrived home from work he might well have felt too exhausted to eat a large meal, or even to eat anything if he had just worked a particularly long shift down the pit. So the ale-gruel would fill him and warm him as he sat drinking it beside the kitchen fire. His wife would already have put his nightshirt to warm, either hanging from the rail above the fireplace or over the back of a chair before the fire. His drink finished, the man would undress before the fire while his wife ran the big brass bed-warmer up and down between the sheets. Then straight into bed, no delay or it was feared that a bad chill would result.

The gruel was made by boiling a good handful of crushed oats in 2 pints of water until it thickened. Then the pan was removed from the heat while a small piece of root ginger was grated in and the mixture stirred well. Meanwhile, an equal amount of ale was brought to the boil and the gruel poured in. A good pinch of cinnamon or nutmeg was stirred in and a large spoonful of brown sugar. Then it was drunk as hot as possible.

An old recipe for Ox-Tail Soup

1 ox-tail	3 oz butter
1 onion	2 tablespoons flour
1 small turnip	3 cloves
1 large carrot	2 pints water
3 or 4 sticks of celery	salt and pepper

Cut up the ox-tail and cover with boiling water. After a few minutes remove and dry. Melt half the butter and fry the meat and the peeled, diced vegetables. Add the water, cloves and seasoning and simmer for 4 hours. Skim as froth rises in the pan. When this is ready, melt the remaining butter in another pan, stir in the flour and allow to brown. Strain the stock off the ox-tail and add to this flour a little at a time and stirring well. Then pour back over the pieces of meat.

Lord Street and Whitechapel Corner in Liverpool, 1908. Eton Suits, Rugby Suits and Cycling Suits are offered for sale in the upper windows of the building on the right; and shirts for 3s. 6d. and 3s. 11d.

Notice the delivery boy crossing the street on the left, carrying his goods on his head. The girl behind him appears to be fashionably dressed for a teenaged girl today in her long skirt and smock top.

The cart carrying milk churns in the foreground was a common sight, for these were the days when milk was taken round the streets to be bought and carried home in the customers own jug.

Peggys' Leg (Liverpool Toffee)

1 lb brown sugar	12 oz lard
1 lb black treacle	4 tablespoons vinegar
1 lb brown treacle (syrup)	1 teaspoon ground ginger
	1 teaspoon baking soda (bicarbonate of soda)

Melt all the ingredients together very slowly, without stirring, on the hob. After a few hours give it one stir and allow to boil until it is ready to set hard. This will take about 15 minutes. Pour half into a well buttered tin and put a small teaspoonful of baking soda into the pan and stir this toffee until it rises white. Pour this light toffee onto the dark and roll it all together while hot then pull it out and twist, cutting off lengths as you like. If you like a good hot toffee you may add a teaspoonful or less of oil of peppermint as you add the ginger.

Liverpool Galantine

8 oz rump steak	$\frac{1}{2}$ teaspoon pepper
6 oz smoked streaky bacon	1 teaspoon salt
4 oz breadcrumbs	a good pinch nutmeg
1 egg	

Mince the beef and bacon together and beat the egg well. Put all the ingredients into a bowl, straining in the egg, and mix thoroughly. Put into a greased basin, cover and steam for 3 hours. Allow to cool slightly then turn out and cover, if liked, with browned breadcrumbs. Store in a covered container and in a cool place when cold. Delicious with salad, or sliced thinly for sandwiches.

A more economical cut of beef can be substituted for the rump steak—shin of beef, etc.

One of the best known of Rochdale's former citizens is Gracie Fields, who, when this photograph of the market was taken in 1910 might have been just round the corner!

I have been told that the trend-setter for checks in shawls was Queen Victoria but she probably never saw one as tattered as that worn by the woman on this photograph.

Lancashire Pea Soup

Peas have appeared in Lancashire dishes for centuries in different forms and in a glossary of the Lancashire dialect published in 1775 was written—

" 'carlings', peas boiled on Care Sunday, which is the Sunday before Palm Sunday. Parched peas or peas fried in pepper, butter and salt, form yet a favourite dish amongst the poorer classes in the north of England on 'Carling Sunday'."

It is interesting to note that carlings were also served in Scotland on the Sunday before Palm Sunday, but in Scotland it was called Car Sunday. The carlings are described as peas, birsled or boiled.

However, in Lancashire peas were always popular at fairgrounds or Wakes when they were sold cooked and by the cupful. They were very often sold from street barrows and could be bought in either the green or black variety. Delicious when splashed generously with vinegar!

Peas have had sacred associations since early times, as for example their traditional use on Carling Sunday, but there is a story that during the cotton famine a boatload of peas arrived and were eaten in delight at the port. This story holds that Carling Sunday is held to commemmorate this day.

A recipe to serve 6 —

12 oz dried peas	3 pints stock from a boiled ham or
2 thinly sliced onions	bacon shank
seasoning to taste	a pinch of dried mustard

Soak the peas overnight in boiling water. Next day throw away the water and put all the ingredients into a pan. Bring to the boil then cover and simmer very gently for 2-3 hours adding more liquid if it becomes too thick.

If ham stock is not available, or a ham knuckle cannot be obtained to cook in with the soup (using water as the liquid), then add 4-6 oz chopped, lean bacon to the water.

A scene full of interest in St. James' Street, Burnley, 1896. The chemist Robert Munns was also the towns' Registrar and this area, known as Bob Munns' Corner, was a popular meeting place for local men. Although the day was apparently hot and sunny, people still wore the thick, heavy clothes of the period, even to hats, shawls and woollen stockings—which made many a leg itch in summer!

Burnley Pie

8 ozs figs	4 oz suet
4 oz brown sugar	6 oz breadcrumbs
2 eggs	1 large tablespoon syrup

Chop the figs and beat the eggs. Combine all the ingredients and mix well. Put into a well buttered basin and cover with several layers of greaseproof paper. Steam for 3 hours. Serve with custard or white sauce.

These quantities make a large, family sized pudding but it can, of course, be made smaller.

Figs feature largely in the old recipes of this north-eastern area of Lancashire and they seem to have been especially popular in the Burnley district.

A Good Carrot Cake

1 cup brown sugar	2 teaspoons cinnamon
$\frac{1}{4}$ cup water	$\frac{1}{2}$ teaspoon mixed spice
1 cup grated carrot	$2\frac{1}{2}$ teaspoons baking powder
$\frac{1}{2}$ cup raisins	$\frac{1}{2}$ cup chopped nuts or dessicated coconut
2 cups flour	1 teaspoon bicarbonate of soda
a third of a cup of fat	1 teaspoon salt
$\frac{1}{2}$ teaspoon nutmeg	

Mix together the sugar, water, fat, raisins, carrots, spices and put into a pan. Bring to the boil and boil hard for 3 minutes. Cool until just lukewarm then stir in the flour, nuts, baking powder and bicarbonate of soda. Mix the salt with 2 teaspoons of warm water and add to the mixture. Stir very thoroughly and put into a prepared tin. Bake 1 hour in a moderate oven 350°. Serve in slices, buttered.

A quiet shopping day on Stamford Street, Ashton-Under-Lyne in 1910.

White milk bread is on sale at one shop, but seven years after this, white bread was to be banned because of shortages due to the First World War. Replacing it was standard bread which included a proportion of barley, rice, oatmeal, beans, maize and later potato.

It would probably have cost the boy the equivalent of £45, in current values, for his bicycle. The first bicycles, known as boneshakers, appeared forty years before this and must really have lived up to their nicknames being made with wooden wheels and iron tyres. They must have given a very painful ride, especially on the unsurfaced roads.

Tripe and Tomatoes

1 lb tripe	4 oz fresh breadcrumbs
8 oz tomatoes	1 pint milk
1 large onion	1 oz margarine

Peel and slice the onion. Put half of the crumbs into a well buttered dish, then a layer of onions, then sliced tomatoes and finally a layer of sliced tripe. Repeat the layers of onions, tomatoes and tripe. Top with a layer of the remaining crumbs. Warm the milk and melt in it the margarine then pour into the dish. Bake for 45 minutes in a moderately hot oven, 375°-400°.

King St., Whalley

Few parking problems in Whalley at the turn of the century. Just one slowly moving cart and one parked minus its mechanism—the horse. The children have obviously not needed to be warned against playing on the road.

Almond Cheese Cakes

8 oz puff pastry	grated rind of $\frac{1}{4}$ lemon
2 oz sweet almonds	2 oz butter
2 eggs	1 tablespoon rice flour
2 oz castor sugar	

Roll out the pastry thinly and line about 18 patty tins. Blanch, chop and pound the almonds very thinly. Beat the butter and sugar hard together and then add the rind, almonds and rice flour. Separate the eggs and beat the whites very stiffly. First add the yolks to the mixture and mix them in well, then gently fold in the whites. Put a teaspoonful of this into each patty and bake in a moderate oven for 15 minutes or less.

Ground rice is a good substitute for rice flour and to avoid having to chop and pound the almonds, use ground almonds. I also find the addition of a few drops of almond essence an improvement.

Bridge Street, Darwen, over 50 years ago, when the men in the photograph had their own idea as to the real purpose of roads—a place to stand and chat.

Pork and Apple Pie

1 oz lard	$\frac{1}{2}$ pint light stock
2 large onions	1 level tablespoon corn-
3 sticks celery	flour
1$\frac{1}{2}$ lb pork sparerib meat	2 tablespoons water
(or other lean pork)	1 large cooking apple
2 tablespoons Worcester sauce	pastry—made from 6 oz
	flour

Peel and chop the apple and onion, chop up the celery and cube the meat. Melt the lard and fry the onion and celery gently until soft. Add the pork and brown.

Remove from the pan and fry the pork until it is brown. Add the sauce and stock, cover and simmer for 30 minutes. Then blend the cornflour and water and stir in. Bring to the boil, season, add the apple and put into a dish. Cover with the pastry and cook about 30—35 minutes, until golden brown 400° Gas Mark 6.

Fashionable Lord Street, Southport probably some-
time between 1890 and 1898. The building of Lord
Street was started in 1825 and only thirty years before
that, Southport was just a collection of fishermens huts.

This leisurely scene shows how ladies usually carried
umbrellas or parasols to protect them from the effects
of the sunshine. It was considered most unfortunate, and
certainly inelegant, to have a tanned skin.

Southport Pudding

4 oz fresh breadcrumbs	2 oz sugar
3 oz suet	1 oz candied peel
4 oz baking apple	4 tablespoons milk
2 oz S.R. flour	1 egg
1 lemon	a pinch of salt
a good shake of nutmeg	

Core the apples and chop very finely, including the
peel. Mix together with the suet and then stir in the dry
ingredients. Grate in half of the lemon rind and add
half of the lemon juice. Bind well together, beat the egg
and add with the milk. Press firmly into a buttered basin
and steam for 2 hours. Serve with custard or lemon
sauce.

A busy market day in Widnes, 1920, in which motor lorries played an important part. This photograph was taken two years after the ending of the First World War, during a time of unemployment and shortage of housing. The Market Hall is seen in the background.

Family Lentil Soup

4 oz lentils	$\frac{1}{2}$ small turnip
2 pints good stock or	1 large potato
water and a ham knuckle	1 large carrot
1 large onion	1 oz butter
1 slice bacon	

Soak the lentils overnight in the stock. If you have no stock, use some water but discard this next day. Peel the vegetables and cut up finely, cut up the bacon. Melt the butter and brown the bacon in this then remove and brown the vegetables. Add the lentils and stock (or the water and ham bone). Bring to the boil, reduce the heat, cover and simmer about $1\frac{1}{4}$ hours. Serve as it is, or sieve if preferred, and sprinkle with chopped chives or parsley.